GOAL SETTING FOR ANYONE

The quick, easy and visual way to build a concrete plan to help you achieve your goals

Contents

Introduction 3

Chapter One: Start Here And Now 4

Chapter Two: Moving On 6

Chapter Three: The Guiding Principle 10

Chapter Four: The "How" Part 13

Chapter Five: Matter Of Time 16

Chapter Six: Get Moving 19

Chapter Seven: Looking Around 22

Chapter Eight: Keeping It Going 28

Chapter Nine: Two Examples 31

Conclusion 35

Goal Setting For Anyone

Copyright © 2019 by Andrew Creager
All rights reserved. This book or any portion thereof may not be reproduced or used in any manner whatsoever without the express written permission of the publisher except for the use of brief quotations in a book review.

Printed in the United States of America

First Printing, 2019

"BEGIN WITH THE END IN MIND"
Stephen Covey

Introduction

The feeling associated with reaching a goal or meeting a deadline can be described as satisfying... even exhilarating. But most wins and successes in life are the results of strong planning and consistency.

Unfortunately, not everyone knows how to build a simple plan to help them reach their goals or targets. No matter your age, if you've ever struggled with creating a plan that has enough information, but isn't too long or complicated, this book is for you.

We'll go through a very simple process on how to create a comprehensive plan that isn't too complicated, and can also fit on a single piece of paper. In fact, you don't even need a computer - a napkin, whiteboard, notebook, or whatever you have to write on (and with) is all you need. You don't need years of experience, or a degree in business administration, to know how to apply what is generally referred to as *'strategic planning'* - but don't let the term bother you; we're only going to borrow and apply the needed items from it.

While writing this short book for my teenage children, it occurred to me that others might benefit from using this method. Even if you are an expert at strategic planning, used to creating large, complex planning documents, you may still benefit by seeing an example of how to fit your thoughts into a small space and easily communicate your plan with others.

Chapter One
Start Here and Now

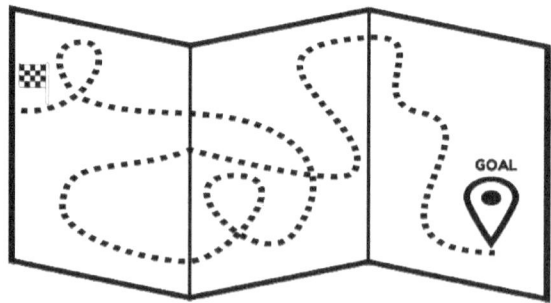

It all starts with a goal. There tends to be a difference of opinion on whether we start with a goal, then add objectives, or start with the objectives, and add goals; I've seen both used interchangeably, but since I prefer starting with a goal, that's what we'll do - feel free to call it whatever you want.

GOAL STATEMENT:

We'll build our plan using a personal example that a student or teenager might create. The goal can be generic for now and we will get more specific in the next sections.

So, let's begin. The goal we'll use as an example is below. You're a student that has your final exams coming up and you want to be prepared. Your last exam didn't go as well as you'd hoped and you want to handle things differently this time around.

> **GOAL STATEMENT:**
> Prepare for final exams

Let's stop here. Really no reason to complicate this. Next, let's look at what needs to occur for us to accomplish our goal.

Chapter Two
Moving On

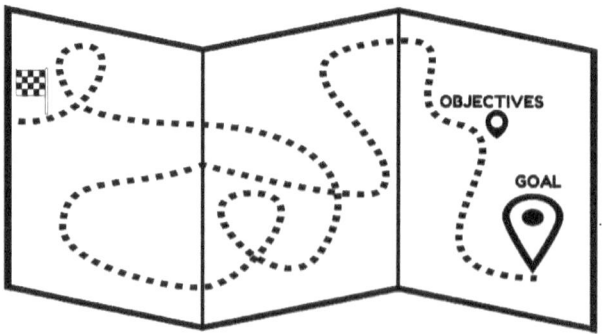

SETTING OBJECTIVES

We started with a goal, preferably a single goal, and we're going to expand our goals into individual components called objectives. Objectives can be defined as actions needed to be completed, in order to achieve our singular goal. This just shows that goals are not achieved just like that, we need to work continuously in order to meet our smaller objectives, which in turn helps us to reach the larger goal.

Objectives support the goal – and it is widely accepted to keep the objectives to no more than 3 to 5. Trust me, this will allow for you to provide a good amount of focus on each objective without becoming overwhelmed. You also don't want to run the risk of creating too many priorities…

Basically, when everything becomes a priority, nothing stays a priority.

Be aware that it is very common for people to get goals and objectives mixed up – which can sometimes lead to confusion; just decide what term you want to use and stick to that.

BRAINSTORM

How do we get our objectives? A common method is to *brainstorm*. Brainstorming is an activity where any and all ideas are noted without any analysis... no criticism, no debates, no fusses; just write down all ideas for major activities that support our goal.

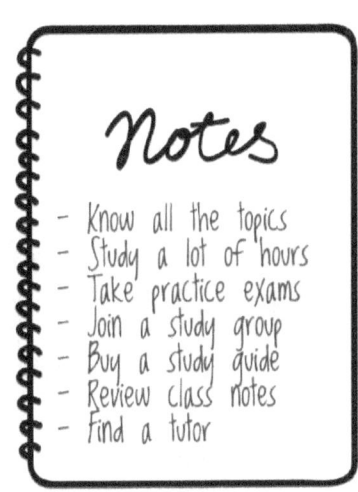

SELECT THREE OBJECTIVES

From our list of ideas, we decide to select three items to become our objectives

Objective #1: Know (study and understand) all exam topics

Objective #2: Take 1 practice exam monthly

Objective #3: Study for at least 200 hours before exams

SMART OBJECTIVES

You may be familiar with the acronym *SMART* when it comes to creating objectives. SMART stands for:

SPECIFIC: in other words, not generic. For example, stating "I want to make more money" is generic, stating "I want to make $50,000" is specific.

MEASURABLE: you are able to present evidence that the objective helps you reach your goal. If making $50,000 is your goal, you'll be able to measure the progress toward your goal.

ATTAINABLE: this is a call you'll have to make for yourself. Back to the "making more money" goal; if your goal was to become a billionaire overnight, I would question the attainability of your goal. However, making $50,000 in a year seems more achievable - this is your call. Just be sure to consider how much effort you are willing to put into reaching your goal.

RELEVANT: is the goal relevant to some end result you seek? Some higher cause? If not, you may want to reconsider the goal you are setting.

TIMELY: your goal should have a due date or some kind of timeline assigned to it to track your progress and provide a sense of urgency with completing it.

Write your objectives below your goal statement... we'll add the time element shortly.

GOAL STATEMENT:
Prepare for final exams

OBJECTIVES:
#1 Know all exam topics
#2 Take 1 practice exam every month
#3 Study at least 200 hours before exam

You can have as many objectives as you like, but we'll keep it to three for our example.

Chapter Three
The Guiding Principle

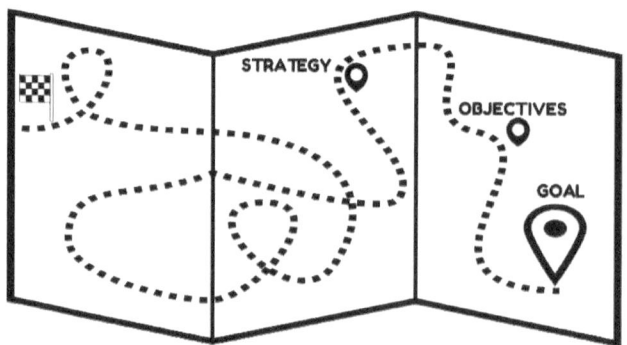

STRATEGY

Strategy - sounds impressive, doesn't it? Sometimes, to me at least, when something gets labeled as *strategic*, I feel as though it needs to be complex, like a game of chess - but that isn't necessarily true. In fact, you can just as easily replace the word with *process*, or *method*. For example, consider a game of chess - it has a single goal: to capture the King; however, the ways (or methods) someone might choose can vary from one player to another. Some choose a strategy of eliminating key pieces, while others may choose a strategy that takes very few pieces off of the board. In short, if you do choose to think strategically about achieving your goal, consider creating a simple, broad statement, that describes the general approach you plan on taking to reach your goal.

So why even bother including a strategy? You don't have to, but I like to because it helps summarize an entire plan with only a few keywords, and, in the next section, we will identify some actions that help communicate the overall plan a little better; this is usually helpful if you are working with a group of people to achieve the same goal.

Looking at our goal and objectives again, what few words would you think of if you had to answer the question, "…what approach are you going to take in accomplishing your goal?"

GOAL STATEMENT:
Prepare for final exams

OBJECTIVES:
#1 Know all exam topics
#2 Take 1 practice exam every month
#3 Study at least 200 hours before exam

Don't overthink it. Let's call the approach we take to meeting our goal as, "daily preparation". So we plan on reaching our goal of preparing for our final exams through daily preparation. We'll add another box (we're splitting this box but will fill it in the section).

Could we have called our strategy something different? Absolutely! We could have just as easily called our strategy, "reinforcing exam content", or "accumulating small amounts of information over time", or anything else related to the goal.

Bottom line, use strategic thinking if it helps you, avoid it if it doesn't.

GOAL STATEMENT:
Prepare for final exams

OBJECTIVES:
#1 Know all exam topics
#2 Take 1 practice exam every month
#3 Study at least 200 hours before exam

STRATEGY:
Daily preparation

And just like a goal has objectives, a strategy has tactics. That's what we'll put in the other side of the strategy box in the next section. Again, add as many as you want; I personally like to keep things as simple as possible.

Chapter Four
The "How" Part

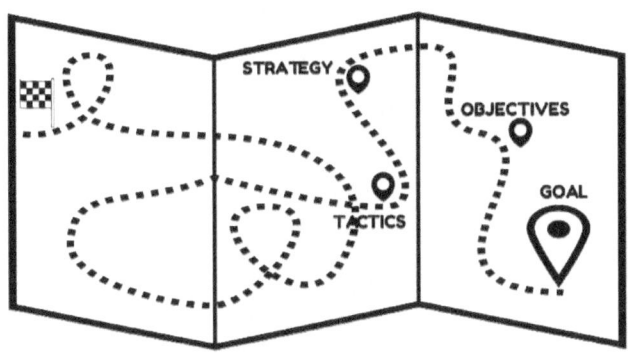

TACTICAL THINKING

Tactics add details to the strategy you choose. For our exam example, do you absolutely need tactics? No, probably not, but it can't hurt. By the way, it is common to mix up strategy and tactics, just like it is easy to mix up goals and objectives. Just try to remember this: if you complete your objectives, your goal should be accomplished; likewise, if you execute your tactics well, your strategy will be successful.

TACTICS AS A TO-DO LIST

Tactics are the to-do's of accomplishing your strategy. Think of it this way

> *Tactics are specific actions taken to support your strategy.*

If your strategy is "daily preparation", then what things, if done, support *daily preparation*? It could be just one item or it could be many items. It wouldn't hurt to brainstorm and come up with a list of tactics - things that support your strategy - and pick the ones that appeal to you the most.

Here's a list of some items (tactics) that I would consider to support daily preparation.

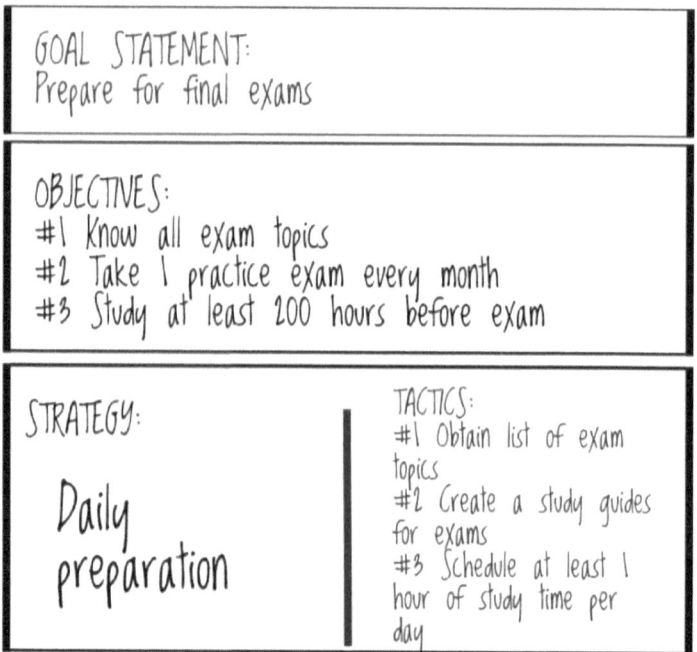

We identified three tactics, listed above. These actions support our strategy of daily preparation to accomplish our objectives, which support our goal.

You could easily have a different strategy and / or tactics and still accomplish your objectives. It's really your call - just do what helps you succeed; also note that though I used three tactics to align with the three objectives, I could have used any number.

Chapter Five
Matter Of Time

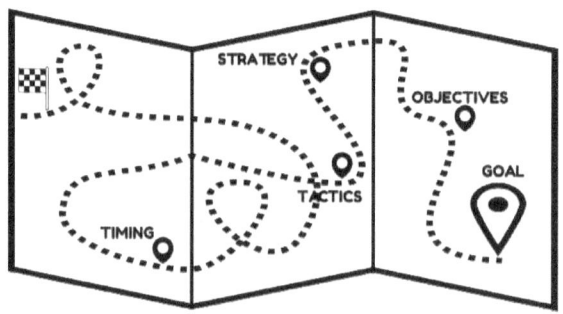

TIMING

This section is the easiest. Let's modify our box diagram slightly to add the time element from our SMART objectives. In doing so, we'll assume it is early January and exams occur at the end of May.

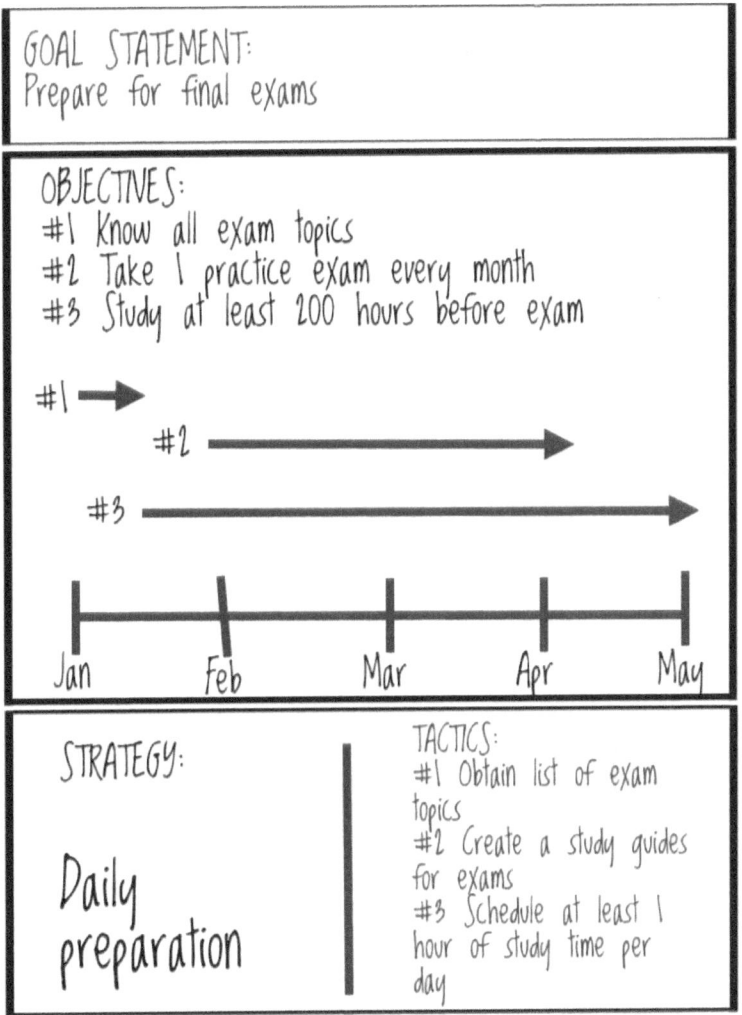

According to our timeline, we are giving ourselves until late January to have created the exam topics list, we expect to start studying immediately following the creation of our study guide, and we plan on taking a practice exam every month until the actual final exam.

One of our objectives, according to our strategy of "daily preparation" is to study at least a total of 200 hours, unfortunately, there are less than 200 days between the start and end of our goal so we will have to double up on the studying some of the days.

By adding a timeline to our objectives, we can budget our time and also track our progress as we work towards our goal.

Chapter Six
Get Moving

The person who says it cannot be done should not interrupt the person who is doing it- Chinese proverb

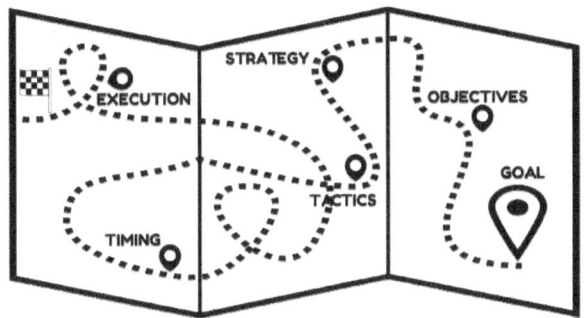

EXECUTION

Since we've made a plan, we might as well follow through on it and succeed; hence, the execution phase, or executing our plan to achieve our goal. How do we execute our plan? Just start - start with objective number one and keep going. Don't wait for a *good* day, or the *right day* - just start.

Sometimes an ounce of action is better than a pound of planning.

A critical aspect of executing your plan is tracking how much progress you make. As you can guess, we'll add another box to our drawing.

Goal Setting For Anyone

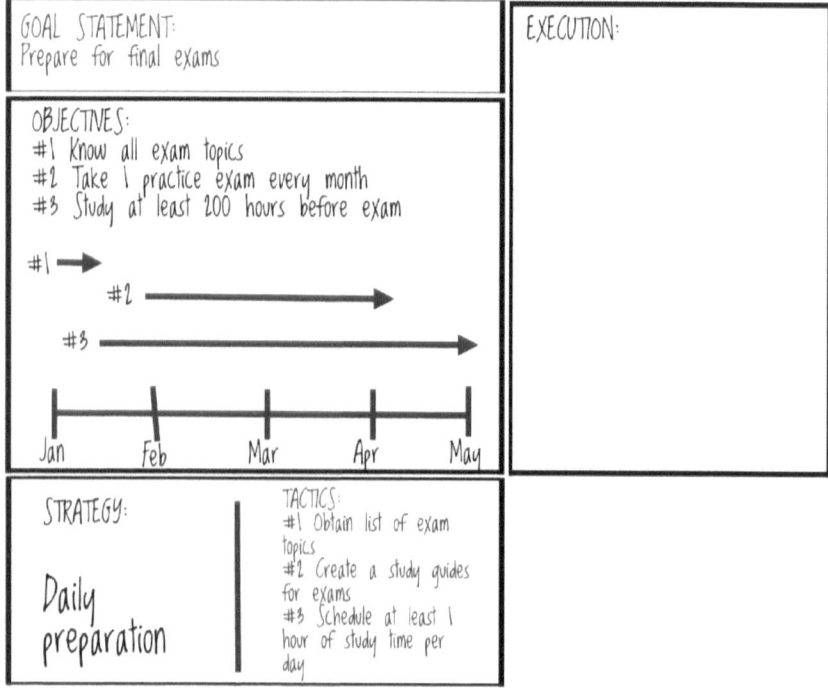

You have a ton of flexibility here. You could draw small boxes to look like a calendar, then check mark the day you study; if you have the software, you could create a simple chart and update it regularly; you could also keep a running total of study hours… do what you like here. The important thing is that you do track your progress.

WHY TRACK PROGRESS?

You need to track your progress for at least three reasons.

1. Motivation - you will probably find it easier to continue working towards your goal if you stay motivated, and since motivation is a frame of mind, it helps to see that you are accomplishing things as you put the time in.

2. Confidence - you will be more confident at the end knowing that you did everything you could to reach the goal.

3. Schedule - scheduling your time will be easier if you have a realistic measure of how much time you have committed to your goal.

For this example, I am tracking my progress as shown below.

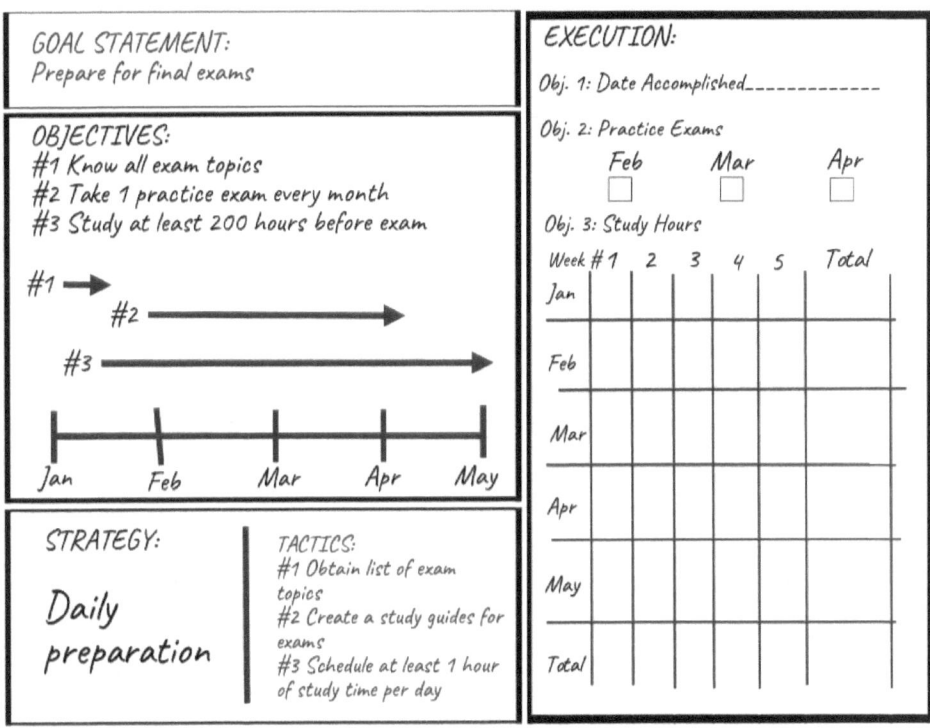

There are a lot of tools for tracking your progress, such as charts or other visuals, but they are not required, or they're usually more complicated than needed.

Chapter Seven
Looking Around

SWOT Analysis

SWOT is short for *strengths, weaknesses, opportunities and threats.* SWOT analysis is a valuable activity that most people, or organizations, engage in during the preparation phase of a strategic planning event. It is usually handled in brainstorming fashion and provides insight to the development of a plan.

IS SWOT OPTIONAL?

Everything in this book is optional - the aim is to help you identify a goal and the necessary steps to achieve that goal. That being said, it certainly wouldn't hurt for you to finish this chapter and spend a few minutes in generating your own SWOT table.

STRENGTHS

In creating your own SWOT table, try asking yourself the question, "what are my strengths"? For our example, your strengths could be that you are disciplined, or that you have plenty of time to study, or even that you are already familiar with the exam material. Take a moment and brainstorm some strengths related to your goal.

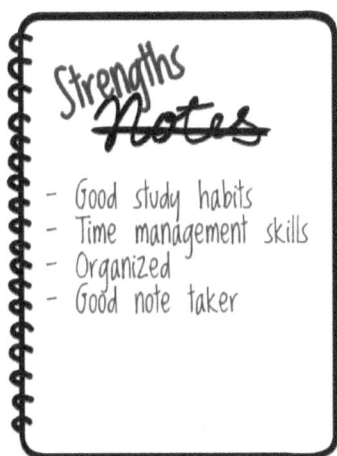

WEAKNESSES

Each of the strengths that you listed above could just as easily be your weaknesses. Maybe you don't have a lot of time to study, or that you know nothing of the exam material. Your weaknesses may even be a bit deeper like, "I lack confidence in myself", or "I'm afraid to ask for help". Brainstorm a list of weaknesses but don't over analyze it.

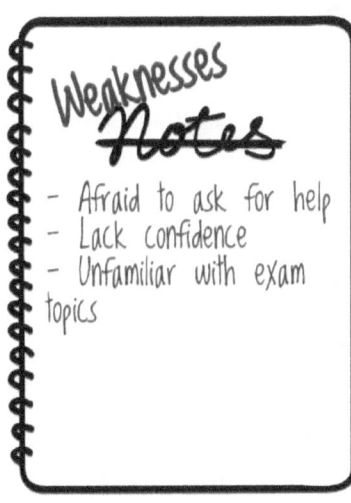

OPPORTUNITIES

Are there potential actions or people that could help you achieve your goal? We would call that an opportunity. For opportunities, maybe your teacher is offering after school time for questions, or maybe you've been told that tutoring is available. Think a little about other opportunities that might exist to help you.

Let's list three: tutoring, after school time with the teacher, and the potential to start your own study group.

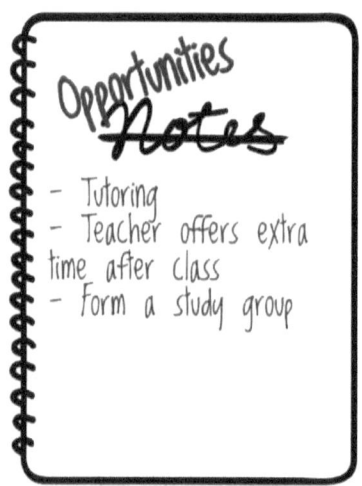

THREATS

For threats, take a moment and think of anything that could get in the way of achieving your goal. What are some of the things that might be a problem or cause you to struggle in achieving your goal? Maybe you have test anxiety (very common!); or you are afraid that you won't actually be prepared for the exam after all your hard work.

For threats, the point is to identify, and list, things that might get in your way, and then come up with a few ideas that will help you avoid those threats. Are you a person that struggles with test anxiety? Trust me, lots of people do and there are resources available to help with that… the main thing is that in order to avoid a threat, you have to first identify it.

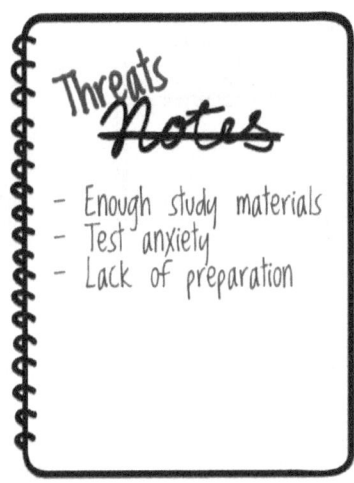

SWOT GRID

If you do decide to create a SWOT table, you could add it to your existing plan in the usual manner - just add another box.

Maybe it ends up looking like this…

Goal Setting For Anyone

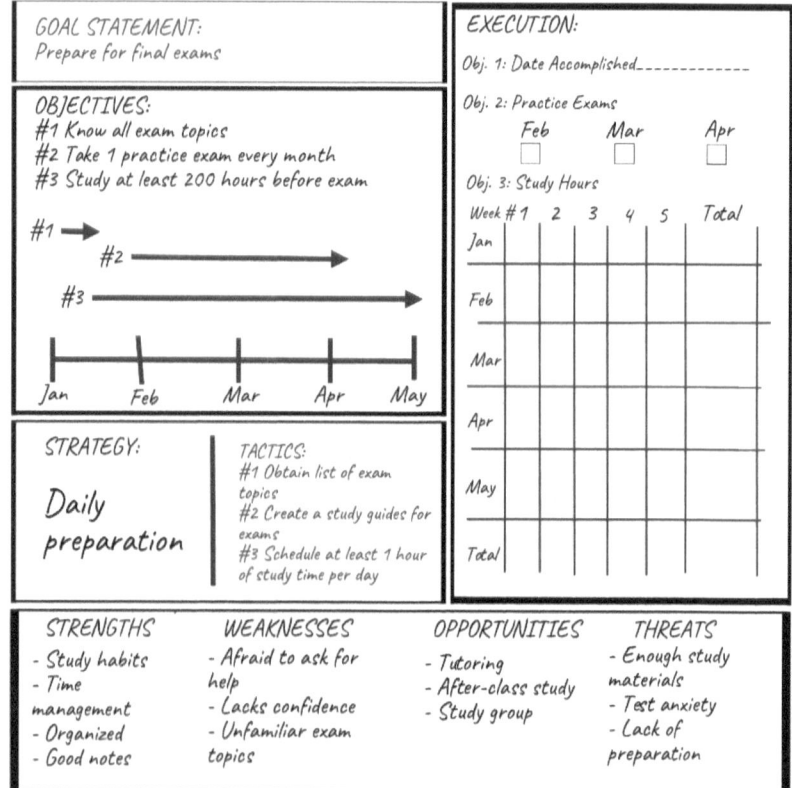

By adding the SWOT to your overall plan you now have a goal, a plan to achieve your goal, and the added benefit of being aware of what can help, or hinder you and your progress.

The process we've covered in the previous chapters can be summarized in the chart below.

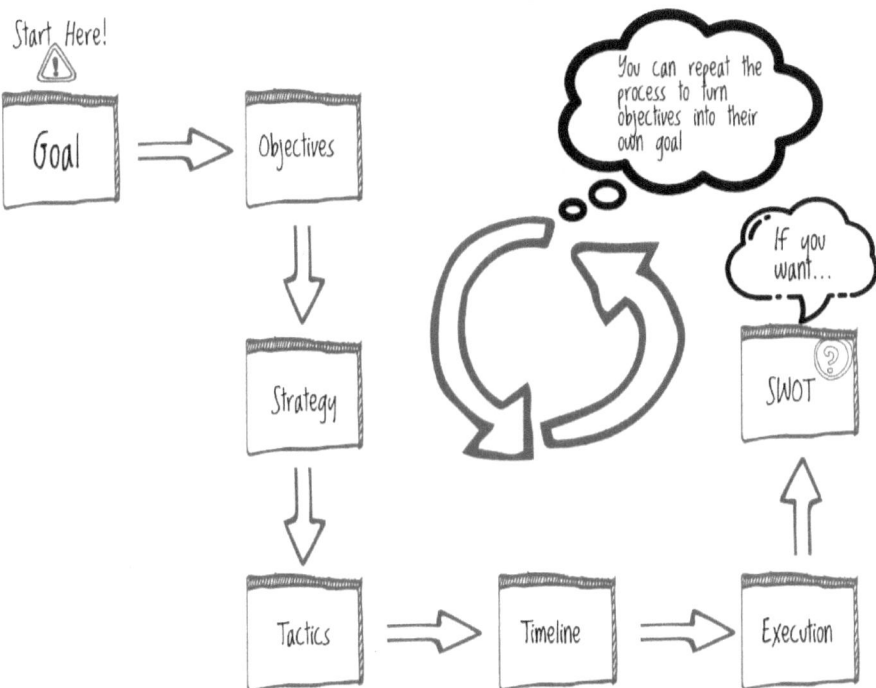

Chapter Eight
Keeping It Going

Let's look at our finished plan again.

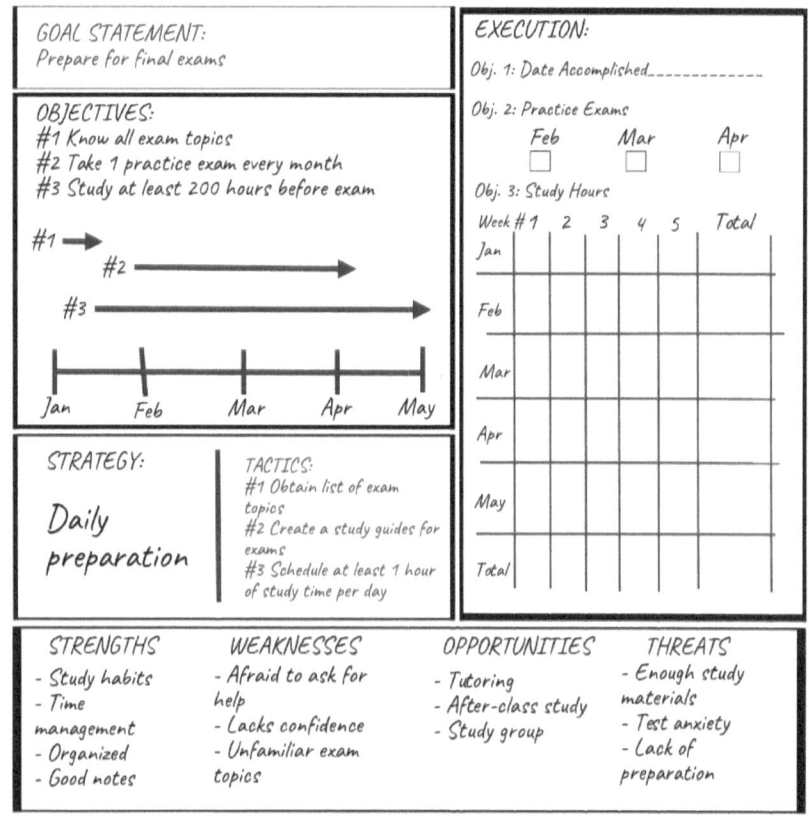

The first objective we've identified is to "know all exam topics". What would happen if, when you start working on that objective, you realize it is actually a lot more work than you originally thought? You could just carry on with it, maybe take some notes or make an outline to help as you go along. But there is another option - you could turn that objective into it's own goal. I'm not saying you need to, or that you would even want to (it is more work, after all), but, I'm just letting you know it is an option.

BUT WHY?

"But why would anyone want to create another plan for an objective that is already mentioned in the first plan?", you ask. Taking an objective and promoting it to a goal is a good way to handle an objective you might want to track in greater detail, and is something I do regularly; and though it is more work, it's not that much more work… you're really only changing a few pieces of your plan. We'll keep strategy, tactics and SWOT the same.

Let's see an example of promoting an objective to a goal.

Objective #1, "Know all exam topics", could involve multiple steps, or you might just want to break it into a few logical steps to aid in tracking your progress. It might look like the example below:

> GOAL STATEMENT:
> Know all exam topics

> OBJECTIVES:
> #1 Meet with your teacher
> #2 Gather study materials
> #3 Have teacher check your study plan

If you choose to promote an objective to a goal, just another box or two to the side of your paper will probably be enough; but feel free to generate as much, or as little, detail as you want. If it is a very involved objective, you could create an entire new layout for it and call it "Goal #2" with its own timeline, etc., this is up to you.

Chapter Nine
Two Examples

I thought it might be useful to provide a couple more examples of goals, and the corresponding first-draft action plan. The first example is business related, the second is a personal goal. Remember not to get too caught up in the details... perhaps you would create very different plans. The important take away from these examples is to show you that we can easily adapt the layout we have been building, while spending our time focused on action, and not over-thinking or over-planning.

Example 1, the business example, has the goal of increasing sales through the fourth quarter of the calendar year – an arbitrary timeline. After brainstorming, the three objectives chosen were

1. Launch a marketing campaign (we want to make sure people are aware of our offerings

2. Offer product discounts up to 25% (an attempt to gain more interest in purchasing our products)

3. Stock extra inventory (we do not want to run out of products)

Again, you could have chosen different objectives, but these support our goal and help us to develop the remaining plan so we can get to work.

Goal Setting For Anyone

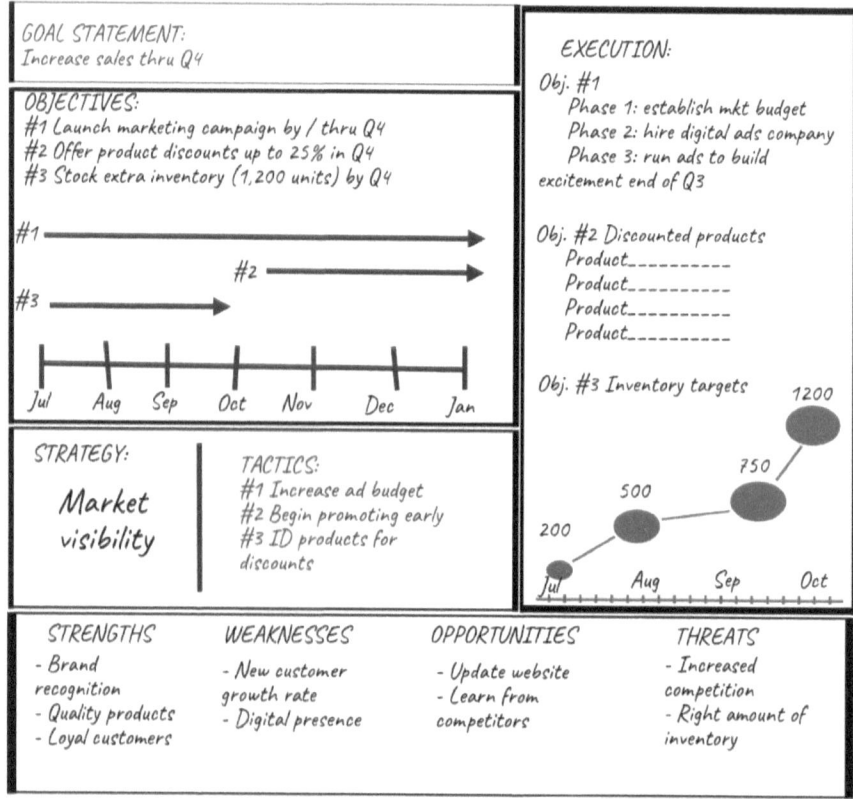

Notice the timeline; we expect the marketing effort to last before the fourth quarter, and through it. This is because it will take time to put the campaign together. We will only offer discounts for the actual quarter we are selling in, and for the third objective, we need extra time to place orders and build up the inventory we anticipate selling.

We call our strategy, "Market Visibility", and it summarizes our general approach to accomplishing the goal. Our tactics could easily include more than the three we listed, but we decided to only list three critical items.

Goal Setting For Anyone

The execution and SWOT sections are set up to support the rest of the plan.

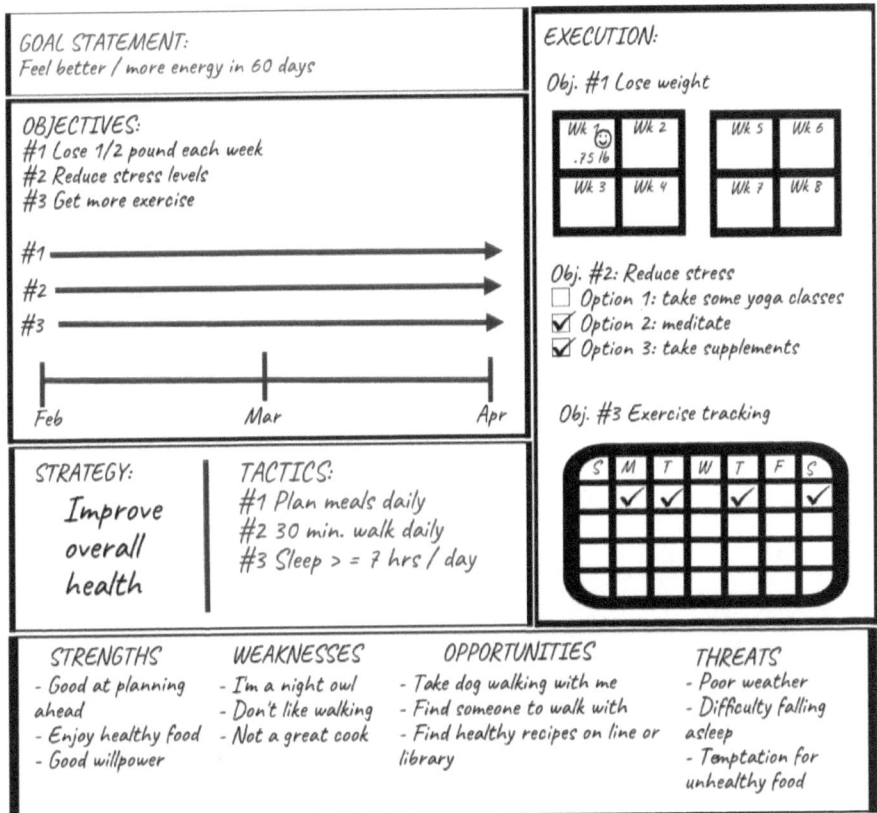

For the second example, "Feel better / more energy in 60 days", we start with a broad goal. The objectives help us better define what it is we think will help us feel better, or have more energy, in the time that we have set. It could be argued that the objectives aren't as SMART (in the measurable category) as they could be, but that's ok because we used the tactics section to add even more details to the plan – don't get hung up on planning details… just get something in place; you can always revise your plan as you progress.

Conclusion

If you made it to the end of this book, good job. I hope this was the easiest goal-setting / planning book you've ever used, and that you are equipped with the necessary tools to set and achieve any goal you have in an easy and visual manner.

The most important thing is that you first have a goal, only then can you move forward with breaking it into the necessary logical steps to successful attainment. Grab a piece of paper and something to write with, sketch out a rough plan, and get going! Good luck!

www.ingramcontent.com/pod-product-compliance
Lightning Source LLC
Chambersburg PA
CBHW030520220526

45464CB00006B/2886